Gallery: The Center for Photography at Steenbock Gallery of The Wisconsin Academy of Sciences, Arts & Letters, Madison, Wisconsin.

Curator: Sarah E.C. Peterson, Appleton, Wisconsin.

Catalog Editor: Judi K-Turkel, Madison, Wisconsin.

[#1] *On catalog cover*

INVISIBLE CHILD. 1967
Street scene in racially divided Bedford Stuyvesant neighborhood, Brooklyn, New York.

Exhibited at Brooklyn (New York) Public Library, 1973; Space 237 Gallery, Toledo (OH), 2009; ATHICA (Athens Institute of Contemporary Art), Athens (GA), 2009. B&W photo 1967, digitized and digitally printed 2009.

Contact info: Judi K-Turkel
3006 Gregory Street
Madison WI 53711-1847
judi@booksthatteach.com
Web site: http:\\www.booksthatteach.com/photos.htm

ARTIST'S STATEMENT

You can't have walked the earth for 70 years as I have, alive to its opportunities as well as its challenges, and feel comfortable with what you see around you today.

Poverty humiliates ever more of our brethren.

Hunger hurts many, many millions of innocents.

Governments ignore citizens who most need justice, homes, jobs—and hope.

Businesses myopically see only a bottom line, but no higher calling.

I fear that when the meek shall inherit the earth, it will be only because the earth, finally, is worthless and we are all equally meek.

Until then—or even hopefully to prevent "then" from damaging the physical, social and spiritual life that once nourished us all—those of us who were singled out to rebel must act wisely and creatively, eagerly and confidently. It is a dismal reality that photographers, writers and other creative artists are left lonely to shoulder this onerous burden, to show life as it truly is and to contrast for others how it could be, should be.

This is the only Earth we have been given to care for. We are the only people who will ever inhabit it. I submit my work as a humble offering toward fixing what needs fixing on it.

BIOGRAPHICAL DATA

Franklynn Peterson was born in 1938 during The Great Depression in a Civilian Conservation Corps (C.C.C.) camp near Phillips, Wisconsin in "The North Woods" of Wisconsin. His family moved toward central Wisconsin via paper mill towns, where his father was a self-taught mill engineer and his mother a canning factory worker. Summers, he spent at Aunt and Uncle Haney's dairy farm near Phillips.

After high school in papermill town Port Edwards, WI, in a class of 24, in 1956 he enrolled in the University of Wisconsin-Madison (B.S. Sociology-Mass Communications) in 1960. An early rebel, Peterson braved McCarthy era politics to join and soon head several radical and antiracial organizations. In 1959-60 he organized and led campus-wide educational forums and anti-segregation picketing at the local Woolworth's in support of students of Greensboro, North Carolina, who were sitting-in down there to protest segregation. This work is often cited as the first northern support action for southern sit-ins.

In 1960 Peterson left for New York City with his wife and infant daughter, and lived on the edge of Bedford-Stuyvesant (Brooklyn, NY) from 1960 until 1975. He returned to Madison, Wisconsin, in 1977.

CONTINUED ON PAGE 24

Our Struggles

In 1965, Peterson was asked by future long-time Brooklyn (NY) Congressman Major Owens of the Brooklyn (NY) chapter of the Congress of Racial Equality (CORE), to document CORE's rent strikes in the Bedford-Stuyvesant section of Brooklyn, NY. A tool created by New York City renters during the Great Depression, rent strikes became the collective withholding of apartment rents in order to pressure slumlords to repair their buildings and to lower gouged rents. As a result of his observations, Peterson joined and became an active member of Brooklyn CORE.

[#2]
HOME SWEETHOME. 1965
Some young dwellers stand in front of their home.

Published in *N.Y. Amsterdam News, Ave Maria Magazine, Sepia Magazine.*
Exhibited at ATHICA (Athens Institute of Contemporary Art), Athens (GA).
B&W negative 1965, digitized and digitally printed. 1965, 2008.

[#3]
COME ON IN. 1965

Published in *N.Y. Amsterdam News, Ave Maria Magazine, Sepia Magazine.*
Exhibited at ATHICA (Athens Institute of Contemporary Art), Athens (GA).
B&W negative 1965, digitized and digitally printed 2008.

[#4]
DOING THE DISHES. 1965

Unpublished B&W negative 1965, digitized and digitally printed 2010.

Personal note: This child's face has haunted me, and the negative was sadly among cherished photos that were stolen by the FBI long ago. Happily, a good print recently surfaced from which I could generate an acceptable digital image for use in this show. I have also asked local media in Brooklyn to help me trace the subject's present whereabouts.   **FP**

BOGALUSA: DAYS OF ARMED PROTECTION.

These photos were taken during two weeks spent photographing in remote, racially divided Bogalusa, Louisiana. There, activists -- many of them Vietnam War veterans -- had previously armed themselves in a successful effort to ward off armed attacks by the local Ku Klux Klan. The aim of those Deacons for Defense and Justice now had metamorphosed into an effort to protect nonviolent civil rights workers. Peterson photographed the Deacons' voter registration drives and one of their two-day marches. During Peterson's visit, the Deacons insisted on providing 24-hour armed protection, and he became lasting friends with the organization's leaders.

With activists elsewhere eager to duplicate their efforts, National CORE Deputy Director Lincoln Lynch was in Bogalusa reviewing their methods during Peterson's stay. Then, when he was landing back in New York, someone looking a great deal like a federal agent attempted to snatch Peterson's negative-filled suitcase before he could claim it. Shortly afterwards, his car was broken into and files of negatives stolen *(see also note to [4])*. Recently Peterson learned that the Deacons had been among the Black militant groups under federal investigation at the time.

[#5] BLACK MOSES. 1967

> **Published** in *Ave Maria Magazine, Sepia Magazine, Newsday*.
> B&W photo 1967, digitized and digitally printed 2009.

[#6]   MOVE ON OVER THIS TIME. 1967
The Black Panther party was just getting organized at the time this march took place in Bogalusa, and its symbol, a black panther, was not yet in common use among African- American organizations.

> **Published** in *Ave Maria Magazine, Sepia Magazine, Newsday. Unauthorized publication in National Review.*
> **Exhibited** at ATHICA (Athens Institute of Contemporary Art), Athens (GA).
> B&W photo 1967 digitized and digitally printed 2009.

[#7] WE'RE POOR BUT WE'RE WHITE. 1967
During a two-day march between Bogalusa and Franklinton (LA), Peterson saw this scene and aimed as he walked.

Published in *Ave Maria Magazine, Sepia Magazine, Newsday*. B&W photo 1967 digitized and digitally printed 2009.

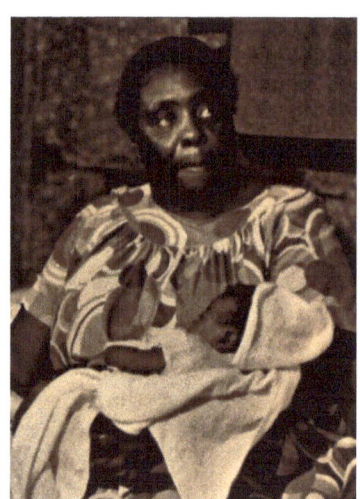

FANNIE LOU HAMER WITH CHILD. 1974

[#8]
MRS. HAMER EARNS A DIVIDEND. 1974
Slicing a meal from Pig Bank dividends.

Published in *Sepia Magazine, Metropolitan Group Sunday Newspapers,* biographical works. B&W negative 1974, digitized and digitally printed 2009.

With just a grade school education in Sunflower County, Mississippi, Mrs. Fannie Lou Hamer was nonetheless employed as timekeeper on a cotton plantation reminiscent of *Uncle Tom's Cabin.* When a SNCC "Freedom Summer" team told her she had the legal right to register to vote, she immediately registered – and found herself unemployed and out of her family's plantation-owned home. The night she and husband "Pap" moved in with relatives, *their* house got shot up. So she worked to register others in Mississippi who'd been lied to about their voting rights. Jailed along with colleagues and beaten there so severely by local police officers that she was left with a permanent limp, she enlarged the territory of her quest for justice, helped form the Mississippi Freedom Democratic Party, and challenged Senator Eastland's seat at the infamous 1964 Democratic Convention in Chicago. Back home, she started a Head Start preschool program that soon became the locality's #1 employer and created Freedom Farms and Pig Bank, both co-operatives that provided the first ecologically and racially sustainable food available to African-Americans living in The Delta.

Previous page, bottom photo: Mrs. Hamer, who had been sterilized by a Mississippi doctor without her knowledge, adopted both formally and informally.

[#9A , #9B] SELMA WASHERWOMAN. 1970
Published in *Sepia Magazine.*
Exhibited at Los Angeles Center for Digital Art, 2008.
Kodachrome 1970, digitally enhanced and digitally printed 2008

Revisiting Civil Rights hot spots, Peterson saw this scene driving between Selma and Montgomery (AL).
Protocol, learned photographing the Movement, demanded that he avoid involving the subject directly
in his photography to protect her from violence. And experience taught him to stay in the car for his
own safety. Yet he owed the woman the courtesy of asking permission.   So he turned off the engine
and air conditioner—despite a hot Alabama sun—so vibrations wouldn't interfere with his exposures,
and held up a camera until the woman nodded briefly. He then waited several sweaty hours for the sun
to change the colors and modeling on cabin, smoke and woman. The reward was worth the wait.

B&W film same day.

[#10]
BOWERY DINER. 1968
Exhibited by Space 237 Gallery, Toledo OH, 2009.
B&W negative 1968, digitized and printed 2008.

Photographing the unfortunate occupants of the streets of New York City's Bowery was a perennial favorite with photographic artists during most of the twentieth century. Peterson's viewpoint adds more than a little irony.

[#11]
BEEN DOWN SO LONG. 1972
Published in *Metro Group Sunday Newspapers*.
B&W negative 1972, digitized and digitally printed 2009.

This coal miner at work near Bethlehem PA is a third-generation miner, and when Peterson met them his son was about to join Dad in the mine. To light this photo, Peterson used the lamps on the hardhats of the subject's three companion workers.

Peterson documented the plight of coal miners working in largely unsupervised small mines in and around the hills of Kentucky. He then captured the rape of the land in the huge newer strip mines run on unprecedented scale by big businesses "out West."

[#12]
DANGER ZONE QUARTET. 1968
Published (segments) in *Sepia Magazine*, *Science & Mechanics*.
Exhibited at ATHICA (Athens Institute of Contemporary Art), Athens (GA).
B&W photographs 1968, digitized into Photo Collage and digitally printed 2008.

The first three successive photos, taken in Central Park, New York City, show a young, jacketed man ready to read amidst gathered protesters, sitting down to observe, and being grabbed for escort to the Station by a waiting Paddy Wagon by two citizens while an Arresting Officer directs the grab. The fourth photo was trained away to one of the group of anti-protesters.

Just after shooting these photos, Peterson was himself arrested and tossed into a cell. These photos would have been confiscated and destroyed by the arresting officer (shown staring at Peterson's telephoto lens in the lower-left image) if the photographer hadn't been alert to that possibility. Stopped shooting almost at once, pocketed the film rolls and loaded blank film into his cameras.

STILL HOMELESS.

In the Twenty-First Century, one out of every four veterans of United States military service is homeless. Currently, one out of every four homeless men is a veteran. Peterson asks: *Are you ashamed for a country that can tolerate such ingratitude? Study this veteran's arm, look at his fingers, and see the pain and humiliation he endures after serving you faithfully in Iraq. Is a cure so difficult?*

[#15]
L.A. VET RESTS 2005
Digital photograph digitally printed.

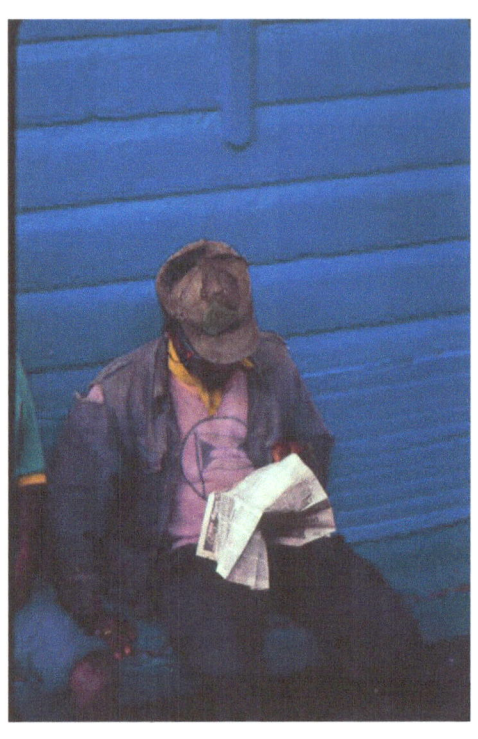

[#13] Previous page, bottom
TOKYO HOMELESS #2.   2005
Digital photograph digitally printed.

[#14] Previous page top
FINAL DIGNITY.   2005
Digital photograph digitally printed.

Toronto (Canada) homeless folks suggested a memorial for their dead to the Church of the Holy Trinity.

[#17] Above left
JAMAICAN STYLE.   1990
Published: *Sepia Magazine.*
Kodachrome 1990, digitally enhanced and digitally printed 2008.

At a Montego Bay (Jamaica) train station bench, Peterson found Jamaica as poor a place to live poor as any other.

[#16] Above right
WEDDED BLISS. 2005
 Digital photograph digitally printed.

A couple calls the Brooklyn (NY) Botanical Garden bench home.

Finding Peace Instead of Strife

CUBA: A RIGHTEOUS EMBARGO? (digital photographs digitally printed)

[#18] Left
CUBAN COMPUTER. 2005
Where replacement parts are embargoed, a scrap of wood does the trick.

[#19] Right
A RED RED CHEVY. 2005
A like-new 1984 Chevy is kept on the road via home-made parts.

[#20] Below
SICK! 2005
Nurse and child after successful diagnosis in a pediatric hospital in Camaguey, Cuba, by surgeons for whom PET, CAT and MRI scanners are affordable but embargoed.

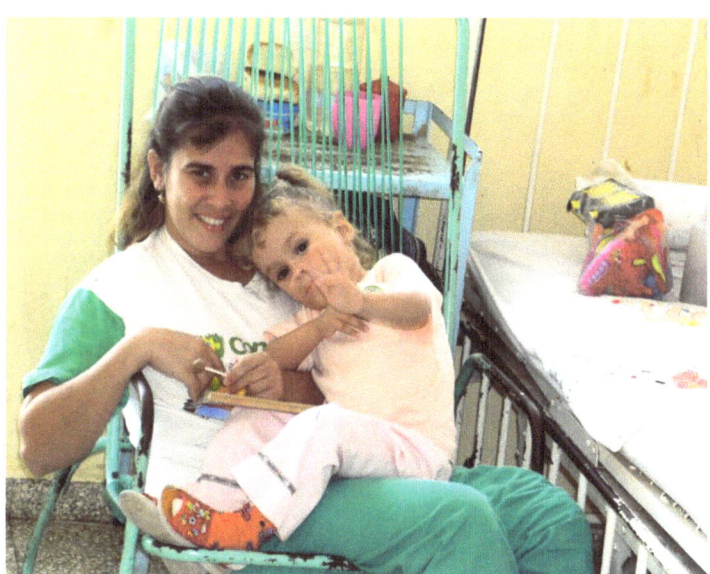

[#21] Left
PEACE. 2005
Digital photograph, digitally printed
Kanazawa, Japan, posed despite language barrier.

[#22] Right
ISTANBUL PARTY. 2007
Digital photograph, digitally printed

[#23] Next page, top
TOMORROW. 1970
Exhibited at Space 237 Gallery, Toledo(OH); ATHICA (Athens Institute of Contemporary Art), Athens (GA).
B&W photograph 1970, digitally enhanced and printed 2008.
Captured on Flatbush Avenue, Brooklyn, NY.

[#25] Next page, bottom left
MAN OF THE STREET IN HIS DIGS. 1974
B&W photograph 1974, digitally printed 2009.
Jesse Jackson at "Black Business Expo" in Chicago.

[#24] Next page, bottom right
MILLENIAL-WATER FOUNT. 1978
Published by *New Woman.*
Kodachrome photograph 1978, digitally printed 2009.

The Havasupai, centuries-long Havasu Canyon inhabitants, take their drinking, irrigation and bathing waters from this river west of the Grand Canyon. From here it flows to the Visitor Campground.

Our Earth or What's Left

EARTH'S JOYS

[#29] Left
DAMN RAIN 2007

Published: *The PhotoPaper.*
Exhibited: International Color Awards, Nominated for Masters Cup, Photojournalism category, 2009.
Digital photograph digitally printed.
Ancient stadium near Kusadasi, Turkey.

[#30] Right
ABOVE IT ALL 2007
Digital photograph, digitally enhanced and printed.

Borrowing concept from the Meterora Monastery atop mountain formation nearby in northern Greece, this home close to the heavens is a private residence.

[31] Above

BOSPORUS OLD AND NEW 2007

Digital photograph digitally enhanced and printed. The Bosporus, Straits, Istanbul (Turkey).

[#26]
SECRET GARDEN. 2005

Digital photograph, digitally enhanced and printed.

Kyoto, Japan.

EARTH'S BETRAYALS

[#27]
ALASKA PIPE DREAM. 2005
Exhibited: "Soap Box 2," American Print Alliance, Atlanta (GA) Savannah College of Art & Design, 2008; "Running on Empty", Athens Institute for Contemporary Art (ATHICA), Athens (GA), 2009; Space 237 Gallery, Toledo (OH) 2009; "Soap Box 2," Hamersley Library, Western Oregon U., Monmouth (OR) 2009; "Soap Box 2," American Print Alliance, Atlanta (GA), 2010; University Art Gallery, Saginaw Valley State U., University Center (MI).
Digital photograph, digitally printed.

[#28]
THE COST OF COPPER.
1976
Kodachrome1976, digitally enhanced and printed 2009.

Anaconda Mine, Utah, miles wide and a mile deep. The silvery caterpillar near left-center actually consists of 25 train cars. The mine closed

two years after this photo was taken and is now an EPA SuperSite, flooded with toxic water. *(More information: see Wikipedia entry for "Anaconda Mine.")*

Seminal Eras, Seminal Photos *(personal favorites)*

[#32]

DOES THE SHADOW KNOW? 1962

 B&W negative 1962, digitized, digitally montaged and digitally printed 2010.

A line in a Spike Lee production on Broadway hit the mark with such reverberation, I paraphrase it repeatedly: "We always seem to make the decisions with the most impact on our lives while we're still in our teens." During my years between 18 and 22, I changed my religion, changed my career, married, fathered a baby, rekindled the Civil Rights movement in Madison, WI, joined the national Movement, corresponded with Rev. Martin Luther King, voted for John F. Kennedy and moved from a home town of 1,100 (Port Edwards, WI) to the home town of millions (New York City).

Like so many apprentices, I went looking for a purpose for my photography other than just making a living. Like most apprentices, I also chased out beauty to find where it was hiding. A beautiful, bright daughter gave plenty of purpose and her presence helped sharpen my instincts. So I caught her tongue against a chalk line on the grass, and then later I documented her mirroring her shadow.

[#33]
LIBERTY DENIED. 1986
Exhibited: Statue of Liberty Rehabilitation traveling exhibition, 1986; "Soap Box 2" traveling show of the American Print Alliance 2008-2010.
B&W negative 1974 digitized and digitally printed 2008.

Chasing world change proved as elusive as chasing daughters' shadows, but in the end it's been more rewarding. Every new assignment, whether from a managing editor or my own volition, resulted in new proofs of how great, as well as how desperate, life can be.

While photographing the now-famous March on Washington in 1963 for an independent film group I had joined, I had the good fortune to stand within speaking distance of Rev. Martin Luther King while he delivered his unforgettable "I have a dream" address.

During the 1964 "Long Hot Summer," I stood a stone's throw from where police and Bedford-Stuyvesant residents first clashed in their three-day bloody, deadly riot that changed so much in New York folks' lives.

A project I founded and funded at Bedford-Stuyvesant's public library, a free drop-in communication workshop for would-be photographers, taught me a lot about fences: Noticing that most of their shots contained fences, I realized it might be because their lives were circumscribed by fences, physical and metaphorical. (See three participants' images, top right.) Startled and depressed, my remedy was to find somewhere where I could show the Statue of Liberty sitting behind a fence. It took the better part of a day to get the image I wanted, but I felt better after that.

[#34]
PRIMEVAL. 2008

Exhibited: Texture show, Aurora Colors Gallery, Petaluma CA, 1908; "PaulaBarr Chelsea International Juried Art Exhibition," PaulaBarr Chelsea, New York NY, 1908.
Digital images montaged and digitally printed.

As Barack Obama's first presidential inauguration was being organized, I took out a recently created digital image and, with mischief in mind, began non-objectifying it. Needing something more for its resolution into expressionism, I juxtaposed more previously manipulated images. The result, shown here, was since submitted to three juried gallery shows, and in all three it found a home.

Shortly after this print started on its way around the galleries, I formally retired from activism. During the Inauguration ceremony, when veteran Civil Rights leader Rev. Joseph Lowery gave all us activists a pass to come down from The Mountaintop, I turned to my fellow Obama team leaders and said, "That sounds so good. It's time that I slow down to smell some roses." And that's where I'm at now.

Settling in downtown Brooklyn, New York, Peterson was quickly able to combine independent mass-media photojournalism with placement in the press of more controversial, more cause-based pieces. He grew from an itinerant chronicler of the Civil Rights movement to a fighter, in print, for Everyman's cause – *Tikun Olam*, helping to save the world. At first, he did the usual: no-holds-barred propaganda just for "the good guys." But because he never veered from strict journalism standards and the honest ethics of his milltown upbringing, he quickly moved onto the pages of large-circulation publications that paid the bills and allowed him to do what he most loved doing. He joined Black Star, a young photography agency created and run by the rising stars of the photojournalism world. Through them, he won remunerative assignments and circulated his photos around the world. His images of the Movement now reached millions in the popular and academic press, in documentary films, in school publications and -- via an international editorial agency -- millions more on other continents.

Peterson pioneered the use in professional photojournalism of small-format cameras that took 35mm film. The camera's tuckable size allowed him to capture intimate, revelatory street scenes as unfolding dramas. He began with an early Leica. Today he prefers a non-SLR digital model, avoiding digital single-lens reflex, having found that mirrors introduce vibrations that hamper hand-held slow exposures.

The artist's friendship with Fannie Lou Hamer, stemming from his University days, led to early and numerous sales to magazines such as *Sepia*, a popular national monthly read mainly by African-Americans, and to *Ave Maria*. a progressive Catholic weekly out of Notre Dame (Indiana). His byline began to appear regularly in the pages of the Sunday magazine section published by the Metro Group Sunday Newspapers, a large consortium of newspapers that included the *Boston Globe, Miami Herald, Chicago Tribune, Milwaukee Journal*, and -- of special interest -- *Memphis Commercial Appeal*, a Sunday newspaper that reached all the way to Sunflower County (Mississippi). In time, he became Editor of *Sepia* for several years, but his true calling was photojournalism.

In the course of his work, Peterson became a trusted creative activist with Brooklyn CORE (Congress of Racial Equality), one of the most militant chapters within the old-guard non-violent racial equality movement. With CORE, he took some of his earliest and most memorable photographs of families trapped in tenements unfit for human occupancy. There it was he met the late Major Owens, who then chaired Brooklyn CORE. Peterson learned about politics by helping to run the first political campaign of that long-time Congressman from Brooklyn.

In the 1960s, Peterson began to deliberately under-expose his Kodachrome photos. The technique resulted in stunning color reproductions with highly saturated colors, but press production required exceptional care on the part of publishers' engravers and lithographers. Only two publications he worked for consistently, *Popular Science* and *Sepia,* reproduced his photos as they were meant to be seen. Happily, today's digital equipment digitizes his under-exposed transparencies so that his highly saturated colors print with great verity.

PHOTOGRAPHIC PRECIS

- Itinerant documenter of social movements, 1960-2008
- Member, Black Star Photo Agency, 1964 – present
- Provider, Bernsen's Int'l. Press Service, 1963-70
- Contributor, Metropolitan Sunday Newspapers, 1964-77.

EXHIBITIONS:
- University of Wisconsin Memorial Union, 1958 (Group).
- Brooklyn (NY) Public Library, 1972, 1973, 1974 (Individual Shows)
- The Camera Company, Madison WI, 1980 (Individual Show).
- Statue of Liberty traveling exhibition, 1986 (Group).
- Dardanelles, Madison WI, 2005 (Group).
- Los Angeles Center for Digital Art, _Top 40_ juried art show, "Selma Washer Woman" 1970, 2007 Digitized Kodachrome digitally printed. April 4-May 8, 2008.
- Watson Studio Gallery, Johnson City, TX. _Abstract Expressions_ juried art show, 2008
- Aurora Colors Gallery, Petaluma CA, _Abstracts, Color and Texture_, September 6-October 12, 2008. "Primeval."
- Athens Institute for Contemporary Art (ATHICA), Athens GA, _Overload,_ September 13-November 2, 2008. "Aflush with Choices," "Cooking Rice Rice Rice Nice," "Cuban Computer," "Buy My Fresh Ikons."
- American Print Alliance, Atlanta GA, _Soap Box 2_ Traveling Show. First venue SCAD (Savannah Center for Art and Design), Atlanta GA, September 25-27, 2008. "Alaska Pipe Dream," "Liberty Denied."
- PaulaBarr Chelsea, New York NY, _PaulaBarr Chelsea International Juried Art Exhibition_, October 16-28, 2008. "Primeval."
- Athens Institute for Contemporary Art (ATHICA), Athens GA, _Running on Empty,_ January 31- March 22, 2009. "Alaska Pipe Dream."
- Space 237, Toledo OH, _Co-Opt_ , April 17-June 5, 2009. 1. "Alaska Pipe Dream,"
- 2. "Invisible Child," 3. "Bowery Diner," 4. "Tomorrow."
- International Color Awards, _Photography Masters Cup_, Nominee, Photojournalism category, 2009. "Damn Rain."
- Athens Institute for Contemporary Art (ATHICA), Athens GA, _Free Press In Free Fall_, September 19-November 8, 2009. **1**. "Home Sweet Rent Strike Home," **2**. "Home Sweet Rent Strike Home #2," **3**. "Vietnam War Protesters Pro and Conned," **4**. "Move On Over This Time," **5**. "Tomorrow," **6**. "Invisible Child." **7**. "Marshall McLuhan What WERE You Doin'?"
- Dozens of private collectors.

- _AWARDS:_
- Oberhausen _Grand Prix_ (shared), Documentary Film Festival, for short documentary anti-Vietnam war film "_12-12-42_," 1966.
- National Conference of Christians & Jews _Brotherhood in Media_, 1967.
- _American Optometric Association_, 1971.

- _ARCHIVES:_
- Manuscript, working papers, and photograph collection, 1960-1978: housed and cataloged at _University of Wyoming_ American Heritage Collection, Laramie, WY.
- Oral history (1978): housed in Oral History Collection, _University of Wisconsin_. It pertains to early years of with civil rights and radical politics as well as career in photography and journalism.
- Photos published in Sepia magazine, 1965-79: digitized and cataloged in Library at _North Texas University_, Denton, TX (Dallas-Fort Worth area).
- B&W Photo Collection, 1964-2000, sold via Black Star Photo Agency: housed and cataloged by _Ryerson University_ (Toronto, Canada) in a collection tracing the recent history of photography and photojournalism.

- Photographic archives of Mr. Peterson's prints, negatives, digital files, will be placed in the Wisconsin Historical Society Iconographic Collection at their request.

On this occasion of both Frank's and my birthday, busy as I have been effectively doing two jobs, I have been thinking about what it all means to me. And it occurred to me what I would probably say if I were called on to deliver a eulogy. And then it occurred to me that the problem with eulogies is that we wait til people can't hear them to say them.

So forgive me if I say it now. If you feel embarrassed there is no reason you need to respond. But I know I don't want to be saying this too late.

Franklynn Peterson, my step-father, is many things. He was a tireless crusader against injustice wherever he perceived it.

A front line soldier in this country's second, unacknowledged war to free the slaves. A political crusader. An activist in many venues and ways.

He is also an artist with a social conscience who believes that art can, and should, critique life and inspire us to thought and action. A kind man and a peace maker too. More than once I've seen him hold his head and temper when all those around him were flaring.

He also has been a devoted companion and support to my mother through thick and thin. Although I've seen them argue and disagree, I've never had a moment to doubt the love that they share.

But to put in just a word or two. My step-father is a good man. One of the best I've had the privilege to know.

And if some day I am lucky enough to have someone say the same about me, it will be entirely due to the example he set me and the things he taught me.

So, on this occasion of your birthday, thank you, my father and I hope that most of my life will be something you will be proud to claim as part of your legacy on this planet.

Love

Jeff

"Everybody's A Customer"

Hu$tleAire

MAGAZINE

www.hustleairemag.com ISSUE 5 SPECIAL FITNESS EDITION

Sweet Capri & Raechelle Chase

Fitnesses Finest

PARENTAL ADVISORY EXPLICIT CONTENT

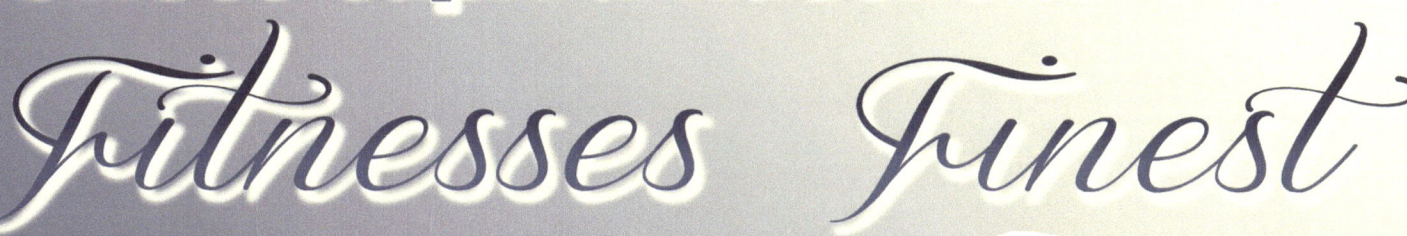

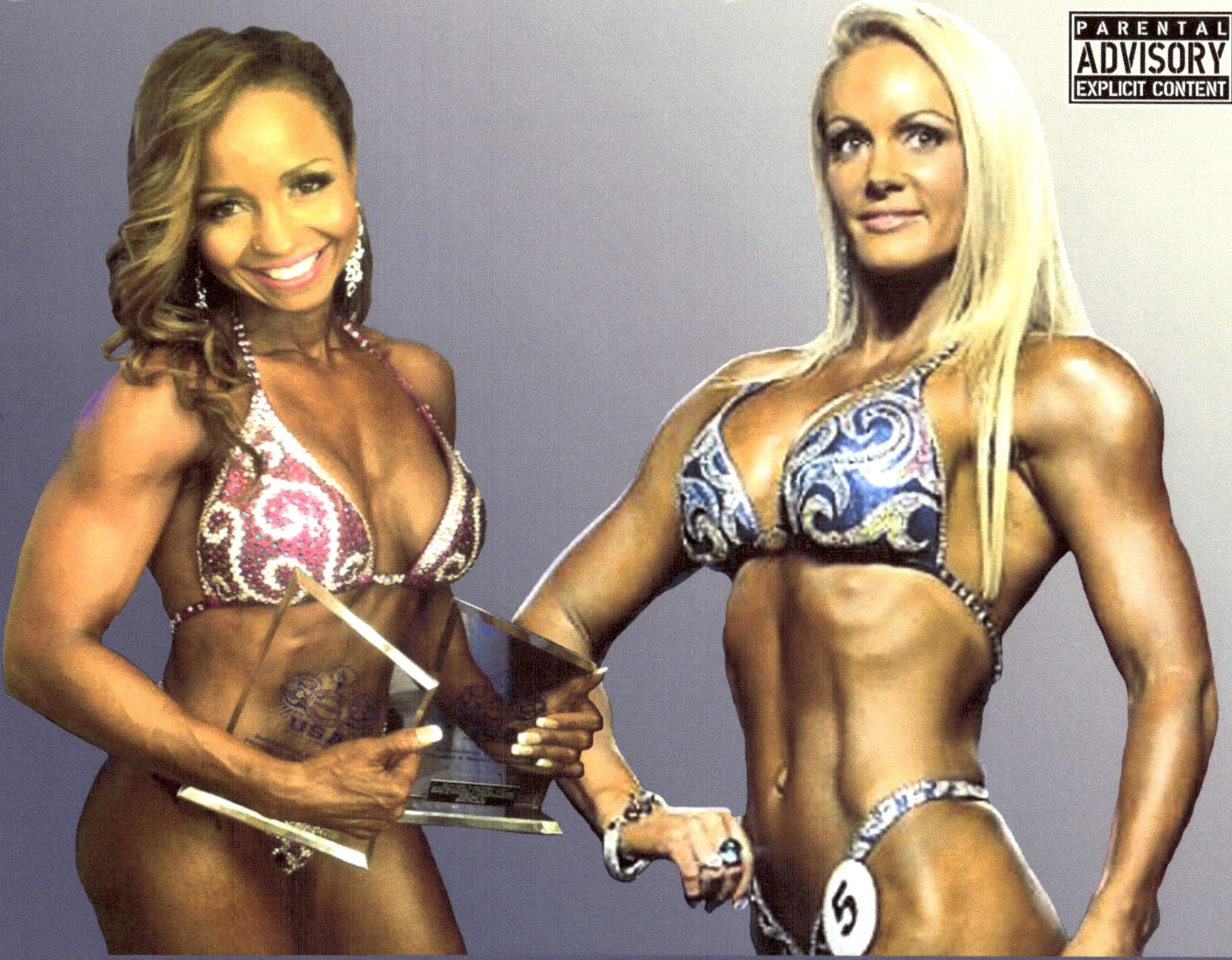

To Build The Best...

We Need The Best.

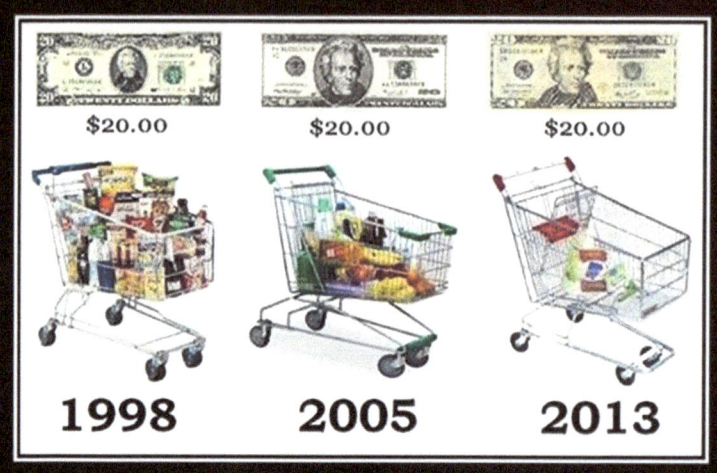

$20.00 $20.00 $20.00

1998   2005   2013

CAN WE STOP PRETENDING IT'S STILL POSSIBLE TO LIVE ON THE MINIMUM WAGE?

CONTENT

MOM SAYS, "ALCOHOL IS YOUR ENEMY."

JESUS SAYS, "LOVE YOUR ENEMY." .... CASE CLOSED.

mgflip.com

TAX SEASON BALLERS BE LIKE...

JANUARY   H&R BLOCK

FEBRUARY   LOUIS VUITTON

MARCH

APRIL   Top Ramen   Oodles of Noodles   BEEF Flav

LMAOBRUH.com